Withdrawal Symptoms

Kaylin Sedhai

THE
OCEAN DEEP

withdrawal symptoms by kaylin sedh

Copyright © 2022 kaylin sedh

For permissions contact: linsedhai@gmail.cor

ISBN: 978-1-957674-12-

Published by The Ocean Deep Publishin

13833 Dumfries Rd, Manassas, VA 2011

Printed in US.

First edition 202

For the Virgo, the Aquarius, and the Capricorn.

I.

I am in love the only way I know how to be
with all of my soul and my mouth in flames
tongue stuck to my teeth for the night
when my name is caught in your breath
let me love you when your hair grows wild
and I am an unrequited lover stuck in my adoration
if I only have you for this moment
please kiss me back when the moon wakes
just choose my window tonight instead
I would never wear my heart on my sleeve
but I will place it in your hands myself

- *la douleur exquise, the exquisite pain*

mama said
to never leave home with my heart in his mouth
but I led him into my dream
with the juice of saccharine red apples gliding down my chin
gripping with my rotten teeth so tight it left bruises,
sitting under the tree where honey drips
down the branches from the rain of God's tears
and I laid my hand down on his chest
but the apple feels like lead in my stomach
when I tell him that I love him.
tracing my fingers around his honey bronze jaw,
I want you to rip my heart out
and make me sing when you touch me;
he is my beautiful boy
but mama said
beautiful boys are like heaven on the outside
and hell on the inside.
we sit together in my red haze dream
where there's no cloud in sight
and the paradise sunset swallows the pink sky
my bronze boy bruises me with his fingers
just like my half eaten rosy red apple
that crumbles in my rough hands

you'll be the person that I'll still think of in 10 years,
on a warm summer day when I'm driving home
when the wind rushes through the crack in the window
and brings me the smell of the sky
it reminds me of the warmth of your shoulder in the evening
the fragrance on the pulse of your throat
and it will be an almost faraway ache in my chest
a vague kind of missing you
like one misses the roughness of a childhood blanket
it'll only sting for a second while I think of you
I would hope that your hair is still the same as it was
I would hope that you're smiling
like you are in the photos on my phone
I'd turn up the volume on my car radio
to drown out your voice singing right beside me
but this song feels like loving someone for a long time
and you might never think of me, or you would,
but then I wouldn't want to know
wouldn't it be easier if you had just never let your hands linger
so much easier if the little things about you
hadn't made it so hard for me to breathe
maybe if I never heard your laugh
that I could recognize in a room filled with voices
all I ever wanted to know was if you felt something too
time leaves like the fog in the morning
when the sun came up too quickly
if only I had enough seconds to make your eyes stay on me
but I just thought that you found the Libra moon beautiful, too
I guess everything was just a coincidence,
and I'll never get to know

one of those days I'll come across you again
amongst the folders stacked in my mind
and it will be painless to flip through the papers
the tickle of the grass against my ankles
wouldn't remind me of you
neither would the warm wet of soil on the soles of my feet
eventually, my soul would give up on yours
and I'd tell myself that I'd be just fine with half of me

I spent a week on Jupiter sucking flowers from your teeth
scraped my knees on the stars climbing down to you
you don't have to tell me anything just yet
always so gentle and afraid with you when they watch
if I love you too hard and the moon dies out with a whisper
you would die in my arms
because of daylilies I planted in your ears
my years-worn soliloquies
finally spilling from my lips onto yours
I'll cover the sun's eyes for just a moment
while I writhe beneath you
you taste like lying in the wildgrass
while the rain drums on my face
my love sticks to your throat
when your tongue swallows me whole
and when the sun has melted to syrup between my fingers
I will trace the lines of my name
I carved into your honey drenched back
sing you back to sleep while your hair curls into my veins
climbing down to wait for the scent of the moon
to swallow your sun love
your tan sugar sky wouldn't touch mine until our next life
what's so bad about the moon kissing the sun?

if you asked me what I was thinking,
I would tell you that I've been wondering how
I have never noticed the stars so much until I met you.
I'm imagining Wednesday morning in the living room
where I kiss you on the cheek and tuck the groceries list
in your pocket cause you'd almost forgotten.

but I'd only tell you all that if
I was dreaming this moment,
so I'll say instead that I've been
thinking about the sun setting
earlier in the fall.

MINI NAAN
BANANAS
THE MOON
GRAPE JELLY
CORE MEMORY
WHEAT BREAD
KISS ME GOODNIGHT

let's pretend that this works for a second,
that you're not leaving me in the cold
rain with the other half of the moon.
the only thing I have is the hope
that I won't feel like this forever
when it's years later and August comes again.
I won't see you in the grocery store
and my stomach won't hurt, and I'm not wishing
that I wrote the list you've got in your hand.

I don't think that we'll ever be in love
but it was nice to pretend.
now it hurts more than I thought it would,
and my heart is leaving with you until forever is done.
I hope that you will be so in love you want to write it in the sand.

but I know that I still love you
because I haven't run out of ways to say it.

sweet baby on the phone line,

we're going to drink apple martinis at dinner in your dining room
and I hope that you find your head in the curve of my neck with
my mouth fevering your fingers. your teeth gentle on my lips and
my inner elbows and in between the curves of my chest.

and this might not be love
but it's warm.

I know it's not love but if I'm hot under the moonlight with you
then it's enough. not that it's nothing special; special doesn't
have to mean forever so we can call it a temporary something
between infatuation and being lonely. guess you could call it
vampirism, the way we kiss at night like we're falling from
the roof but we die under the sun just to eat the moon and live
again. so we set fire in the dark and blow away the smoke in the
morning. sex on your tongue and pink in your cheeks, hair wet
on the nape of your neck. tiny permanent tattoo for a short term
accord when we got drunk down in Myrtle Beach. I care a lot,
and it's not enough to see your eyes in the morning but it's okay
with me if we just play pretend once the stars flicker back on.

champagne doesn't taste like new beginnings
as the songs say they do but we're fine.
we'll be fine if we don't think about it all too much.

I woke up with a fever on the 13th of August,
and today I'll finally tell my mother I'm staying home.
because I have been lying through my teeth.
loving you so hard it's seeping out of my skin,
and I'll just hope that I love you less when you go.
but you're just so soft on my skin that I can't help it,
and when you slip through my fingers I'll die in my bed.
oh, I know that it'll bruise me til I can't move,
but come kiss me in my room before you go
and rest your cheek on the top of my head,
even if you've never loved me the same way.
I know it's only like one loves the soil beneath their feet;
you get sick of the wet warmth after a moment.
but I have loved you like you'd love the color of the sun
setting against the ocean cause I'll never be able
to take my eyes off you no matter how hard I try,
and I'll get salt in the cracks of the skin on my knees.
I haven't been counting the days but it's going to be 105,
between when I've woken and when I will die.
I'll smile at you on that Tuesday morning
when the sun is shining in my eyes,
and I'll never let you know any more.
but I'll still laugh until I can't breathe
when my lungs have already given out in my chest.
I'll be pronounced dead in the sand
and the doctor will say my heart had eaten my brain months ago.

for how long has the night called to you,
lips forming my name against your window?
for how long have you listened, salt beneath
your door and the windowpane, moon stuck
in your ears? for how long will you pretend?
laying there in the silence, to wallow in the
slow sticky autumn and know the truth but
not chase it because it is different. to live in
the arms of familiarity because it is easier.

for how long will you tell yourself that you don't want to be
selfish?

October felt like one hell of a year
started like a soft conversation
while the rain drums on the window
watching the moon simmer in that curve of your shoulder
only the rare glance swollen with something I thought was there
I wish I could have said that you only almost had me
but the way your eyes widen is so familiar
your voice is a song that I've heard before
how is it that a name can crack against my teeth
and I could taste it in my fingertips
the way you looked in purple lights under the moon
something so simple that could bring me to the ground
to say almost wouldn't be even half of it
you had me pulled by the strings of my heart
strummed it so well like you'd known how to play for years
I thought the chords were all right
but I guess I don't have perfect pitch
my lovely little Aries moon
you didn't fall in love in October but I did
and it will never be anyone's fault but mine
to think that the sun would ever fall for the burnt out star

although I haven't been keeping track of the days,
there was a sting in the air today, and I already knew.

it's the last month of the year and I'm still dying from the heat,
but I just didn't want to step a foot into December
when I'm still thinking of you like summer never left;
so give the warmth back to me
before our frostbitten fingers snap apart.
I wish that I was back in Leo season but here I am in the cold,
and I can't tell you anything without saying
what you don't want to hear. didn't you know
that I fall in love with anything that thrives in the sun?
didn't you know that I have always loved so hard
for things that didn't happen? but I'm out under the grey clouds
in the weather that can't really figure it out either,
and winter has never snapped my bones like this before.

there is no one to forgive because December
has left the sun lodged in my throat and it froze overnight.

funny, how New York City in the wintertime makes me think
of you even when the closest we got to a trip together was just
a stretched-thin conversation about going back to my place. we
never even spent a full season together but I swear to you that
we've been here before, senior beach week spent in a hotel room,
nights where I was studying the lines on your face instead of
the lines in my textbook. you are the only language I have ever
really known and this explains why I could never make sense
of what my heart was telling me until you opened your mouth,
and then I just knew. so ask me if I am in love, there won't be
a such thing as a short answer. I feel as if in this life we have
never intertwined, but we've brushed and that is just enough.
it's been too long. and I have started to forget how your voice
sounds but I find it again when I spend a night stuffing my ears
with odes that sound like the wet warmth of a summer evening,
a half-swallowed October afternoon where I sat down heavy and
listened to my heart shatter. I wish that I didn't have to shut the
door so hard to make it all seem final because all I'll ever want
to be with you is gentle. and all this time I have wondered if you
ever found yourself in the hopeful but sour words that stayed
steady flowing from my tongue even if I had only been looking
at your back. I don't think I will ever know.

-      *it's not a love song if I don't recognize you in it*

I do still listen to what the stars have to say to your sun sign today. Virgo, leave the window open just a crack tonight. Virgo, speak to the moon and don't tell anyone what she told you to do. sweet Virgo, did you notice the amethyst ring, calling you and telling you to come home? listen closely. the wind has given you two choices and you are too selfless to make the one that you really want. you will find your way back just seconds too late because you finally noticed that you don't really like the way this name is slippery in your mouth. the journey is almost two months long no matter which way you turn, and by then the body would have gone cold days ago. dear Virgo, take a closer look at the tea leaves at the bottom of your cup. I think the earth has been trying to tell you something for years.

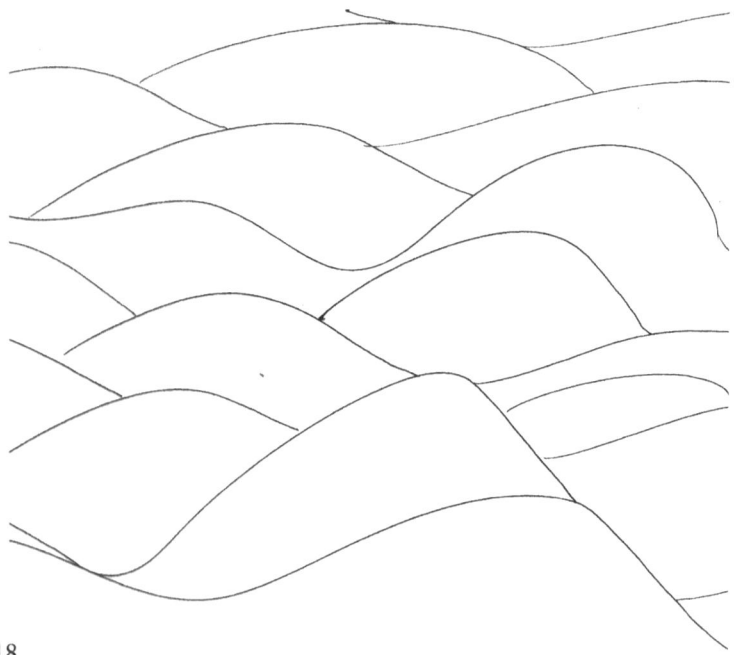

II.

thought that we were catching honey on the sun the other day after weeks of you just staring at my mouth for what seemed like hours on end. but it's been 5 minutes since we said goodbye and you're already leaving on the train. I've been crying your tears for you even though I couldn't do it for myself and now I am bone dry. so I guess that this is the kind of love that kills. knew from the start that you didn't care but I could've sworn there was a second where you let the syrup trickle down your throat. you did for one second and that was more than enough for me. but then you sat next to me and acted like you didn't know. either too good to be true or too bad for me to be on my knees just like this.

I so quickly swiped honey with a finger and devoured it
but forever ends more quickly than I thought
and it ripped a hole clean through my chest.
you were sugar in a bowl, the candy jar on a counter,
and I was a child in a candy store during the purge.
love me like syrup and sting me like salt in the wound.

yesterday I found your warmth
in the remnants of the fireplace.
now I'll spend the rest of December
with my cheek in flames, and my tongue
branded with your name. I want that inch
between our shoulders and I want to watch
your chest rise across the dinner table.

I want everything from afar so I can only just
feel the heat, but I can't let myself scald
my fingers on your skin. come back home
to me for Christmas and set my body on fire
again, just one last time. I would rather burn
in silence than hear those songs of yours that
I still don't know, because it will hurt even more

if I knew your middle name or the street
you grew up on or what you want to do
when you leave home. if I knew the smell of
your mother's cooking or where you go for the
holidays or the childhood things that you will
never leave behind or the time you set your
wake-up alarm for or how hot you like your showers.

and god, if I knew the taste of your
mouth and the movement of your hands
when you love, I would never let you go.
this year, give me the gift of never knowing
the small things, and I can walk away like
I didn't feel the fire against my skin.

instead, I will tread water in the cold
and freeze myself over until I don't know
what warmth is. so please stop living
in my dreams when I feel the coldest.
I just want to be snowed in this winter.

so you've begun to store what little you have of his things
six feet under, right next to our bones (convenient).

don't you think it's time to dig yourself out of that grave?

the soil has been swept with leaves five times over,
it's already Christmas and the headstone is snow dusted.
I don't want my body to stay in the ground until spring
so let's speed up the grieving process.
being buried alive is getting a little cramped and it's been months
since the last time that you gave yourself space to breathe.
you made guest rooms upon guest rooms and I think
this time you spilled out of our chest for good.
I know that you might love him but you're rotting again.
but once all's said is done is it going to be worth it
if you've loved to your limits and he's still out of reach
and you are still cold in the ground
with lungs full of graveyard soil

you've got me for the third time this week and,

I'm sorry. I love you. *I know*. but it's cold. *I know*.

please don't get me your coat. but you will and I'm sinking into the snow because it's just a fucking coat and all you ever do is know things without saying much else. I don't want your stupid coat and I don't want your fingers in my hair and I don't want your toothbrush next to the sink. I don't want to but I need you to hold me like you never did. I'm sorry I could never tell you that I love you. I'm sorry that I still can't say loved because it's never going to be in the past for me. I'm sorry that you haven't left my head for a hundred days.

I love you. *I know*. but you don't know, and it's cold. *I know*. but our flowers wilted from my frostbite before they even began to bloom. you're sitting in the sun and I don't want your hand-me-down love but I need it.

I've been getting too many signs to leave you in last year so I guess this is it. Co-Star astrology notifications with too-perfect timing, and too many puzzle pieces coming through the doorway trying to fill the space you left. there are no more angel numbers and I've given up on swallowing rose quartz before bed. my fingers are slipping while the rest of my life waits for me on the canyon floor but you grasp my hands so tight. still dreaming of you telling me that you love me, and maybe it's almost sixty degrees on the first of January because I tucked a little bit of that summer day in between my teeth and the inside of my cheek. now the warmth is splitting my mouth wide open but I tell myself that I can't have dreams of you anymore. I can't look for you in onscreen smiles or flowers in the wind. this isn't like when homecoming rolled around and I just pressed my heel in the dirt for one night. but now I'll have to say that it's all new beginnings and leave you in the year where summer never ended for me.

January is slow,
and it bites like the cold with an aftertaste of homesickness.
you pretend there's not a you-shaped hole in my chest when I
stand in front of your door,
but you just shrug your jacket over those shoulders and ask,
aren't you cold?

and anyone would grow ten different earths from those words
but I have loved you deep enough to know you are just sweet
and dumb. I wish that you had the common courtesy to walk all
over me and turn me cold and hard towards you. but you walked
with me, not on me, and so I split myself open every new moon
and taught reproduction to my heart. but that was then, and this
is now. January is tired of a lot of things and I have wanted to
stop loving you for as long as I can never remember. but January
remembers, January remembers the times I wrote you down on
the inside of my pillowcase, sang forgiveness to a mouth that has
spoken too many apologies to mean anything, asked the traffic
lights if you love me more than you did yesterday morning.

January asks, casually and half-awake, if I can place my beating
heart on the table as I leave.

I don't know if you are finding this whole
or in pieces. I don't know if we still keep in
touch. I don't know if I ever did make it to my
18th birthday, and if you smiled as big as I hoped
you would when I blew out the candles. all I can say
is I hope you remember me like I remember you. I
hope you think of the possibility on that slick summer
day that just barely glanced off my fingertips. I hope that
when you think of poetry, you will still think of me and just
wonder. if I only live in the back of your mind, then it will
be more than enough. I hope you find me in pink cheeks and
the last bit of ink in a dying pen and scraped-empty containers
of rose vaseline. I hope that you find me only in the memory
of happiness. I hope that we have loved each other enough in
silence to watch from afar. I hope that by now, you've realized
why I could never bring myself to say goodbye to you on
Monday.

I wish that you wouldn't forgive me when I apologize.
and that you are not soft and kind when you speak to me
as you are.
as you've always been.

hey, it's me, just checking in. ~~*have you thought about me recently?*~~ *I hope you're doing well, and sorry I haven't reached out in a while. I've just been* ~~*thinking about you too much so it was too hard to pretend that I wasn't*~~ *really busy lately and keeping up with a lot of things at once.*

but keep me updated on college applications! ~~*I still haven't stopped seeing you in my dreams and it's killing me*~~ *and let me know when you're coming back to visit!* ~~*I love you and it's killing me*~~

I have named you many things. the rain caressing the cheek of my window, ripe warm earth the peak of summertime. a love letter that will never find where it's meant to go, the moon and sun sharing the sky right after sunrise. I don't know if you've ever lived in Oregon but you belong there, your spontaneity and patience, the quiet slope of your nose. there's a college there that's named after you and I would have gone there to make it my home away from home, and that's why I name myself the things I do, silly and reckless and dumb with the things I've done because of you. walk thousands of miles and paint all the stars your favorite color. stare into the drawer at my job because someone who has your name hasn't picked their order up in months. *I cannot stand seeing your name everywhere like that when you should be called so much more.* so I have named you many things. code names with my friends like muscle tee, pretty boy, Virgo number four. blueberry lemon chapstick, every single tall tree, the sound of cicadas just as spring closes her eyes. sweet baby but I never got to say that you were mine.

I wrote a book. I wrote essays about the curve of your eyebrows, I directed a movie about conversations between two moles on the nape of your neck when you are fast asleep, I found the eighth wonder of the world climbing mountains on your back.
and I forgot my address because I had been calling you home for so long that I don't know where I ever could have lived before.

I am sitting here with this book and you don't love me.
you have heard me speak about you for six months and you are still frustratingly unaware. but I don't know if I prefer you not knowing to the gray sky of a look you might give me if you did know. for this long, I have been listening to people speak, and I found you in every sigh, every mention of summer, every love poem. I heard every word and you never listened and now my ears are raw and tired.

I don't even know if you have moles on the nape of your neck; I was always too afraid to look. and I am so tired of pretending not to love you. even the corners of the universe listen to the way that I love you, they smelled the smoke when I set myself on fire with the warmth of your skin. after this, I know that I will still love you forever but at least I know that I never meant to.

February has never been this cold.

things are different,
your warmth next to my shoulder now makes me shiver, and I've
become cautious around you, tiptoeing around the curls of your
hair. I want to wallow in your summer forever but I have things
to do, places to go. and people say that everything happens for a
reason but I can't think of one for this. there's no lesson here, not
found in the sweat on your back, the slight pink of your face. you
have kept me warm for so many cold months but you've grown
too small in the distance.

I should have seen it coming.

it's simple; I'm tired of writing about a kiss that never happened. shoulders that brushed were just shoulders that brushed, and I don't want to write fiction anymore. the phone call was just a phone call and you happened to be the one thing I hoped you wouldn't be. a lesson to learn.

I will never give my heart away like this again and maybe this time I mean it. I think that you still have pieces of it stuck in your teeth.

my firefly, stuck in the cusp of summer.
I don't think you understand, I don't think you ever will. if I love you this hard will it be enough for the both of us? will you understand?

the way my soul almost rips my chest and jumps across the room to you. the way I dig my heels in the ground against your pull. I ache for you like you will never know. I think I know everything about you and I wish I knew nothing. I want to put your flecks of summer in a suitcase and send it on vacation; let me have this summer to myself. and I would miss you but you were never mine to miss.

I tried to write about somebody else last night and I didn't know how. I don't breathe the same when you're not around. and I am so sorry, but I can never move on. I only became a poet when you looked at me like that.

III.

we are in Georgia and you got that tattoo
on your ankle that you've always wanted
remember, the honeybee?
we are sitting across the table from each other
and I know that we will never be more than this

and I swallow the sun
because I have always burned for you
I sat there and stared at your back for years
and I know it better than the layout of my home

this is home, found in me and you, quietly burning,
and just you, and the matchbooks in your palms.

if not now then when?

when I was in your room for the first time, I dreamed that it was mine too, and it was easy to change my clothes in front of your mirror. it was sixty degrees and I shut the windows; three in the afternoon and there was so much we said in the comfortable silence. I got home and my mother asked if we were a thing now.

I said no, because you were February and I was June, and you capture the stillness of what happened and I write the words that should have been said.

I said no, because you wear this particular shade of blue and then it's June 23rd below a cool summer sunset and I can't remember anything before you.

I said no, because you are the first woman I've ever loved and it's the last months before you leave me for Providence Springs and I think I've been holding this in my chest since we started playing pretend.

we should talk about Italy. the conversation we had in your truck on the hour-long drive to the beach. the sun in the roots of your hair and the lines on your face when you smile. can you still call it conversation if our lips really had no space to talk?

I would do it again. I will do it again.

this is different

you weigh the same as me and you dress like me,
you love like me and you talk like me,

and we know just as much as each other

and writing about you is different
my words have no teeth

I don't have to draw this out to say I love you
it's been there for four years now
and the world stood still, waiting
for me to just say it out loud

I will love you until the last light burns out.
I will love you even if we don't cross paths
for the rest of our lives
and I will love you if I see you again in the April rain.

after it happened
I sat in your car and looked at you.
your eyes were on the road
but if you had glanced at me,
I don't think that you would have seen me.
and there I realized that we were just friends in a car.
and there I realized that I had kissed you first.

you're not counting the hours or the miles
that it would take to get to my college from yours
but I am. so what's it going to be?
twenty minutes or seven hours?
now or forever unspoken? and am I asking you,
or am I asking me?

Tuesday I love you like the birth of spring, the phone ringing in the other room with no one to come pick it up. I think that you could have loved me back, if we met in the afternoon, if we met during the spring, if I said something differently, if I never cut my hair, if I let my hand linger for one second longer.

I will still care for you, when I see your smile lighting up a phone screen or across the parking lot, even when it's not for me, even when I am a rest stop in the path of your life and you are the happiest ending I could have asked for. you say that I can do anything and I wonder why I couldn't love you enough.

Tuesday comes and I think of you but I try not to love you. I ford all my love across the river and I pick a color for my prom dress that you didn't tell me to wear. I know I'm going to die without you so I'll start pretending now. I know that I never had you, so I have nothing to lose.

needing you,
in the creases of my palms,
and the pages of a good book

I find myself wondering about your hair and the way your
eyeliner looks today and the way your eyes smile before your
mouth does

I find all of the humanity I thought I lost, in you

I go to bed and see you in a dream
I built a house for you there,
and I drink your tea,
and pick fruit from your trees
in the backyard,
and you read me poetry
on the bank of the river
you tell me of the time your father
spit cherry pits across the room
you tell me of blackbirds on the moon,
and spring's cold morning breath
bringing goosebumps on your shoulders

April smelled like the birds' wings
skimming the tops of the water and we watch
they wander off and your words are faltering
as the mornings go by faster and the sun
pushes itself slowly, wearily through the sky

this is the routine, things we are used to
grass in the morning and midday poetry
the heart of the Occoquan at 4:30 in the afternoon
soon this will be something we used to do

the worst kind of grief is found here
in things and people that exist and live strong
grieving the *before*. grieving the buried imprints
of our hands in the sand and grieving, forever,
the space next to my shoulders that wasn't there
until we left our little dreams behind for good

realism

you cut your hair,
I call your cell phone and hang up before you have the chance to say anything. I knew you'd change without me but it had only been a month and I wasn't ready. I think about how in a few years, the hairs on your head will be ones I've never seen before. and you look good, the nape of your neck quietly marvels in new light, and now I think about people I thought I'd loved who cut their hair. never looking quite as good as you with their heads lighter.

the last time I saw you, you said hello with a smile. and our shoulders were touching and I wondered if you could hear what my heart was saying, being this close, being this quiet. this would have to be enough.

I got your name tattooed
on my bottom left wisdom tooth,
running my tongue along the ridges
in my mouth so I never forget

you are so good
all I want to tell you is that
I have weighed your heart in these palms,
I have placed it in my own chest,
I have heard the words you wait eagerly
to say. and you are so good.
you look down at me and your hands are ghosts,
hesitating above my shoulders, now my waist,
settling for your own sides
it happens in seconds, and you are so good

turning corners of brick walls the next weekday
and you are too good at saying hello
I stare at the coffee in your cup holder,
your teeth as you smile above me,
cradling your face, you lick my teeth,
and you are so good

I push back my wisdom teeth appointment,
I set it for a thunderstorming hot summer day
where I sweat you out like a fever
and wonder why my mouth tastes like metal
I smell the storm, like heat and wet grass,
the shape of your birthmark in the nimbostratus
I make it rain so hard that I'll forget this forever

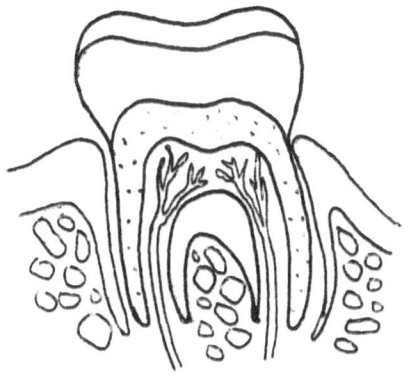

in the spring, I promise to sew myself new skin
I take my tulips and show my palms to the sun
steadying my shivering shoulders
and placing my ear against the sky;

I am the one who always remembers, hesitant fingers on my back
                and the little things. I am the one who takes it to heart,
                    the whispers against ears and the quick stolen glances,
                        with your eyes widening before you look away.
                            I am the one who reads your face like a book.
                                I am the one who bears the brunt of it all,
                                    I am the one who pleads guilty.

but the first person I love is not the only one,
maybe it lingers in my soul for good but I think
it will stay with yours too, the half written story,
the apple that was too high up to reach,
a reminder of what could have been.

for all the nights I spent in withdrawal without you
days that I gazed out the window looking for
what I thought was home, folding my love,
quarantining myself into my heart
a six-month long fever with the chills

    I am the thing that wanders and never knows, clinging to you
            like the dew to the grass in the morning. I am the fever,
            I am the cusp of spring, the ice melting with humid rain.

in the spring, I promise to fossilize this love
and sprinkle the bones into the ground
to let the soil soak up the last of it
watching, as I leave your story in the cold
and straighten my back when I walk,
for the first time, without cruelty or regret
without love or hate, and I walk, for the first time,
warm.

about the author

born and raised in woodbridge, virginia, kaylin sedhai is a 2022 graduate of charles j. colgan sr. high school and is heading to virginia commonwealth university. *withdrawal symptoms* is her first chapbook. in her free time, she likes to go on walks, be with friends, listen to music, and write more poetry.